REA

DO NOT REMOVE
CARDS FROM POCKET

ALLEN COUNTY PUBLIC LIBRARY

FORT WAYNE, INDIANA 46802

You may return this book to any agency, branch,
or bookmobile of the Allen County Public Library.

THE WINDOW

THE WINDOW
New and Selected Poems

DAHLIA RAVIKOVITCH

translated and edited by
Chana Bloch and Ariel Bloch
with a foreword by Robert Alter

The Sheep Meadow Press
Riverdale-on-Hudson, New York

Copyright © 1989 by Chana Bloch and Ariel Bloch.

All rights reserved. No part of this publication may be reproduced or transmitted in any form or by any means, electronic or mechanical, including photocopy, recording, or any information storage and retrieval system, without permission in writing from the publisher.

All inquiries and permission requests should be addressed to: The Sheep Meadow Press, P.O. Box 1345, Riverdale-on-Hudson, New York 10471.

Cover design by Lillian Elliott
Design and typesetting by Keystrokes, Lenox, Massachusetts
The book was composed in Mergenthaler Bembo

Library of Congress Cataloging-in-Publication Data

Ravikovitch, Dalia, 1936–
  The window : new and selected poems.

  1. Ravikovitch, Dalia, 1936–   —Translations, English.
I. Bloch, Chana, 1940–   II. Bloch, Ariel A.   III. Title.
PJ5054.R265A22   1989   892.4'16   88-34896
ISBN 0-935296-81-6
ISBN 0-935296-82-4 (pbk.)

Printed in the United States of America

CONTENTS

Foreword by Robert Alter   ix
Translators' Note   xv

The Love of an Orange (1959)
On the Road at Night   3
The Tearing   4
The Commandment   5
A Wicked Hand   6
Clockwork Doll   7
Painting   8
A Small Woman   9
Delight   11
The Land of the Setting Sun   12
Night Sorrow   13
Someone to Save Him   14
Around Jerusalem   15
Behind the Rain   16

A Hard Winter (1964)
Requiem after Seventeen Years   19
Dust   20
Magic   21
Time Caught in a Net   22
Distant Land   23
Heartbreak in the Park   24
Trying   26
Trying Again   27
Heron   28
Hills of Salt   29
The Raging Waters   30
Mahlon and Chilion   31
A Hard Winter   32
Abuse   33
They Told Me to Bring   34
A Great Tremor   35
The Blue West   36

The Third Book (1969)
Surely You Remember   41
Two Songs of the Garden   43
Australia   45
Now the Moon   47
Vanilla   48
The Marionette   50
Pure Memory   52
Imagination is a Boundless Thing   53
The Horns of Hittin   54
Pride   56
A Dress of Fire   57
A Personal Opinion   59
In Chad and Cameroon   60
How Hong Kong Was Destroyed   61
In the Right Wind   63
The End of the Fall   65
Even a Thousand Years   66

Deep Calleth Unto Deep (1976)
Day unto Day Uttereth Speech   71
Midnight Song   72
Poem of Explanations   73
Sand   74
Deep Calleth unto Deep   75
In Jerusalem   76
Like Rachel   77
King over Israel   78
Impoverishment   80
From Day to Night   81
The Sound of Birds at Noon   82

Real Love (1986)
Iddo Wakes Up   85
The Glass Pavilion   87
Little Child's Head on the Pillow   88
The Beginning of Silence   89

Cinderella in the Kitchen   90
The Finish Line   92
A Declaration for the Future   93
Rough Draft   94
Requiem   95
Gadi in Richmond   97
Blood Heifer   98
You Can't Kill a Baby Twice   100
On the Attitude toward Children in Wartime   102
Hovering at a Low Altitude   103
New Zealand   105
It Will Certainly Come   107
Birdy   109
Light and Darkness   110
The Window   112

Notes to the Poems   113
Biographical Notes   117

FOREWORD

The most remarkable of Dahlia Ravikovitch's poems seem to well up suddenly from depths of visionary perception. Sometimes the speaker of the poem views the objects of vision from a narrative frame, as a story that happened once upon a time ("The Tearing," "Painting") or that could happen ("How Hong Kong Was Destroyed"); sometimes she plunges into the quicksilver current of the experience ("Delight," or, in a more explicitly sexual mode, "The Raging Waters"). Still other poems, especially in the last three of her five volumes of verse, imagine the visionary revelation from a certain distance as a longed-for redemptive irruption into the bleakness of ordinary existence. That note is struck in certain recent poems—"The Beginning of Silence" is an example—and in earlier ones such as "Pure Memory," which ends with these lines:

> How many days, years,
> thunderstorms
> have we waited for one
> pure memory
> to break from the depths of the earth
> bright red as a poppy.

Elsewhere, Ravikovitch sees rather than hopes for such sudden flowering of color and rapturous (sometimes frightening) intensity: "The treetops blazed, the light couldn't have its fill,/molten in the waves, it set the river on fire,/would have swallowed my head too, like a golden orange." Or more pastorally, with a primitivist's stress on primary colors: "The woods of green sheep flowed down the slopes/and the sea below splashed and turned blue in the sun./Clouds opened white, like water lilies." In some instances, the intensity of these visionary moments swells to a violence that bursts the seams of the everyday world: "First the lights go wild,/the colors start from their frames./Stars plunge from their height like epileptics."

Underlying this openness to the excitements of epiphany is a child's sense of wonder and terror, a child's perception of the world as a place of uncontrollable forces, and a child's dream of storybook escape. The Hebrew that Ravikovitch uses in her first two volumes of poetry is an apt vehicle for such a sense of reality precisely because of its ostentatiously literary, uncolloquial character. With its highfalutin diction, its archaic turns of speech, its abundant biblicisms, often conjoined with rhyme, it evokes the rather stilted language of Hebrew children's literature (which, at least until recently, has corresponded more closely in style to Edwardian children's literature than to any contemporary English counterpart). Chana and Ariel Bloch's consistently deft translations, which for the last three of Ravikovitch's five volumes breathe in English the very life of the Hebrew originals, wisely avoid any attempt to mirror the obtruded stylization of the earlier poetry. Even so, Ravikovitch's aroma of children's verse has been preserved in the English versions:

> The way is so long
> and the new moon's like hammered tin,
> and who can tell gold
> from a bit of tin
> that's worth a worn penny.

Ravikovitch's third volume of verse, published in 1969, with its flaunted anti-title, *The Third Book,* is a turning point in her career. Rhyme and quasi-balladic forms give way to free verse, and from the opening lines of the collection ("After they all leave,/I remain alone with the poems") the language, with rare exceptions, is emphatically colloquial in diction, idiom, and grammar. The impulse to reach for an exotic elsewhere is satisfied in two memorable poems, one historical ("The Horns of Hittin") and the other a fantasy of the Orient ("How Hong Kong Was Destroyed"). For the most part, however, the new realism of the language is joined with a new definition of the poet's task as the exploration of the grayness, the protracted disillusionments, the anguish of daily life as an adult. T.S. Eliot's use of ironic colloquial monologue had been an important influence among the Hebrew poetic modernists of the 1950s, when Ravikovitch began writing, but it is only a decade later that she herself reflects this trend. A few of the most striking poems of *The Third Book,* like "A Dress of Fire" and

"Even a Thousand Years," are explicit monologues, while other strong pieces in the volume, such as "Vanilla" and "Pride," suggest colloquial address even though the object of the speaker's attention is not her own experience but another person or people in general.

It took imaginative courage for Dahlia Ravikovitch to make this move from the visionary to the quotidian, and it was not without artistic dangers. In avoiding the allure of that early world where "Larks were whistling,/starlings hung in the clouds,/and the skies were filled with ravens shrieking," she has sometimes fallen into the trap of too unmediated an expression of unadorned misery. The least inclined of poets to any affirmation of the here and now, her spare colloquial mode at times leads her into a bare statement of how aching and bereft she feels in a grim world, and the occasional transposition of this plight into the third person scarcely alleviates the problem.

This desire to achieve a kind of naked verbal engagement with what is seen as the awfulness of everyday reality prepares the way for the political poems Ravikovitch wrote in the wake of the Lebanon War. The Israeli invasion of Lebanon in June 1982 was a watershed for much of the Israeli intelligentsia because it was the first war widely viewed in this group as neither defensive nor preemptive but as a wanton military adventure, exacting a gratuitous toll of Arab and Israeli lives. There was an outpouring of protest poems in the months after the Israeli invasion, among which were quite a few by Ravikovitch, who had never before written explicitly political poetry. It is fair to say that the ones included in this volume are urgently sincere expressions of a revulsion of national conscience shared by large numbers of Israeli literary intellectuals. Otherwise, the poems scarcely transcend the simplifying clichés of self-consciously engaged literature, and American readers will easily detect the parallels with anti-war poetry of the Vietnam era: the heavy-handed ironies, the inevitable images of murdered children, screaming women, and so forth. The familiar Ravikovitch fantasy of imaginative escape to some exotic bourne turns up among these poems ("New Zealand") as sour flat statement devoid of poetic elaboration.

The one political piece that seems to me to live as poetry with peculiarly disturbing power is "Hovering at a Low Altitude," a poem that begins with ominous portent ("She won't live out the day,/that girl") and ends with the first motion of the rape and murder of an Arab shepherdess (perpetrator unspecified). What turns this potentially sensationalistic material into a haunting poem is the tense relation of the female narrator, watching the action from the safe distance of "a low altitude," repeatedly announcing, "I am not here," as the unwitting victim is about to be seized by the assailant ("I haven't seen a thing," says the narrator) in the final lines. The image of low-altitude hovering over an atrocity is an obvious but nonetheless effective emblem of the situation of the ordinary Israeli, knowing but choosing not to see certain terrible acts perpetrated by other Israelis, or even in the name of the nation; more generally, it is a parable of the moral untenability of detached observation in any political realm. Psychologically, the effect of the poem is more complicated because the woman poet, through the indirection of her distanced narrator, also identifies strongly with the victim of the rape. I hardly mean to suggest that Dahlia Ravikovitch's future as a poet is adumbrated in this poem, but it is worth noting further that "Hovering at a Low Altitude" is an inversion of one of the recurrent structures of her previous work. For coordinate with her chafing against the confines of the quotidian and her thirst for visionary intensities is a fantasy of sailing off or flying away to a splendid never-never land. This theme is in the foreground of "Distant Land," of "The Land of the Setting Sun," and, most brilliantly, of "The Blue West":

> And a sun will shine for us blue as the sea,
> a sun will shine for us warm as an eye,
> will wait until we climb up
> as it heads for the blue west.

It seems that for the grimmer Ravikovitch of the 1980s, there are no longer any fairy-tale sky-vessels that might whisk her off to the ends of the earth. The attempt to fly away in the end comes down to a low hovering over a landscape of disaster to which the fictitious observer is painfully unwilling to acknowledge her connection. Thus a moral critique of escape, or a representation of the impossibility of floating detachment, becomes the subject of Hebrew poetry's virtuoso proponent of escape's enticements. That, too, is an imperative of poetry in trying times, even for so vivid an imaginist as Dahlia Ravikovitch.

ROBERT ALTER

TRANSLATORS' NOTE

The Window: New and Selected Poems offers a representative selection from the work of Dahlia Ravikovitch over a period of almost thirty years—from her earliest volume of poems, *The Love of an Orange,* published in 1959 when she was 23, to *Real Love,* which appeared in 1986.

In 1978, the Sheep Meadow Press published a collection of Ravikovitch's poems, *A Dress of Fire,* translated and edited by Chana Bloch with the assistance of Ariel Bloch. For this new collection, the two of us have worked as collaborators, revising the 39 earlier translations—many of them extensively—and adding 38 others, primarily from Ravikovitch's first and last books. Some of these poems have appeared in the *Graham House Review, Delos, Modern Hebrew Literature, Reflections* and the *Tel Aviv Review.*

In making this selection, we have departed from strictly literary criteria in one instance: we have included a few political poems of protest first published in the Israeli press during the recent war in Lebanon. These poems, which Ravikovitch herself calls "newspaper verse," have aroused much debate in Israel, and we judged that they would be of interest to an English-reading public.

We are deeply grateful to Stanley Moss for his close reading of the manuscript and his inspired suggestions. Every translation in the book has benefited from Chana Kronfeld's impressive learning and her critical eye. Shirley Kaufman commented on the poems with her customary sensitivity and incisiveness. Eamon Grennan and Diana O'Hehir helped find graceful solutions to a number of problems. We were fortunately able to consult with Dahlia Ravikovitch, who elucidated puzzling lines.

Finally, Chana Bloch is grateful to Mills College for a Faculty Research Grant, and to the MacDowell Colony and Yaddo for green pastures and still waters.

Chana Bloch and Ariel Bloch

THE LOVE OF AN ORANGE

ON THE ROAD AT NIGHT

On the road at night there stands the man
who once upon a time was my father.
And I must come to the place where he stands
because I was his eldest daughter.

And night after night he stands alone on the road
and I must go down to that place and stand there.
And I want to ask the man how long will I have to.
And I know, even as I ask, I will always have to.

In the place where he stands there is a fear of danger
like the day he was walking along and a car ran him over.
And that's how I knew him, and I found ways to remember
that this very man was once my father.

And he doesn't tell me one word of love
though once upon a time he was my father.
And even though I was his eldest daughter
he cannot tell me one word of love.

THE TEARING

Then the stranger walked away,
a twist of ivy clung to his shoes,
a scarf was knotted around his neck,
and the wind gored him.

Larks were whistling,
starlings hung in the clouds,
and the skies were filled with ravens shrieking,
the terror of sunset, a blaze
of rose.

And a wisp of straw lifted in the wind,
flashed and glinted like one of the stars.

Light and shade were like clusters of grapes
black and green, dangling from a twig.

And a wisp of straw that lifted in the wind
twitched and was trapped between the ravens' wings.

And then that stranger walked away,
a twist of ivy clung to his shoes,
a scarf was knotted around his neck,
and the wind
gored him.

THE COMMANDMENT

> *Six hundred thirteen commandments*
> *were given to Israel,*
> *and seven to the Sons of Noah.*
> *Even the dead must fulfill a commandment.*

And the dead man came home again
to tell his children about his death
so they would not be shocked to hear
the dreadful word.

Never was there among the dead
a man who did such a thing.
Go look at the graves of the dead and see
if anyone's done such a thing.

And he sat with us, he didn't stir,
seven days of mourning.
For how could he alone find peace
while we were all in grief?

And he told us about his death,
explaining it over and over again,
for he imagined that was the way
for us to be consoled.

And even though he deserves to rest,
he'll come back whenever we call,
won't ever close his eyes to our pain,
he'll carry his equal share.

Days of mourning, years without end,
whenever we call to him,
whenever the grief overwhelms us,
he'll surely have to come.

A WICKED HAND

Smoke swirled through the slanted light.
That night my father hit me hard.
Everyone laughed who saw him do it—
that's the truth, nothing but the truth.

Smoke swirled through the slanted light.
My father slapped the palm of my hand.
He said, It's the palm of a wicked hand.
That's the truth, nothing but the truth.

Smoke swirled through the slanted light.
My father stopped hitting me.
The wicked hand grew fingers again
but its deeds live forever and ever.

Smoke swirled through the slanted light.
Fear singes the wicked hand.
My father stopped slapping me
but the fear lives forever and ever.

CLOCKWORK DOLL

That night, I was a clockwork doll
and I whirled around, this way and that,
and I fell on my face and shattered to bits
and they tried to fix me with all their skill.

Then I was a proper doll once again
and I did what they told me, poised and polite.
But I was a doll of a different sort,
an injured twig that dangles from a stem.

And then I went to dance at the ball,
but they left me alone with the dogs and cats
though my steps were measured and rhythmical.

And I had blue eyes and golden hair
and a dress all the colors of garden flowers,
and a trimming of cherries on my straw hat.

PAINTING

The woods of green sheep flowed down the slopes
and the sea below splashed and turned blue in the sun.
Clouds opened white, like water lilies,
and we were still girls.

And one of us had eyes everyone loved
and we all envied her till we forgot.
And one was tall and blonde,
and whatever they asked her in class, she always
knew the answer.

And I would go out in the sun to the nearby field
and love the clouds and dream up stories about them,
and I had plenty of time to think about sorrow
from the first day of gray autumn till the end
of yellow summer.

A SMALL WOMAN

A small woman made the world
her bed
—that great big world.
And it wasn't unknown to the world
that a small woman
was resting on him.

And he grew grass into her lap,
wrapped her body with stalks of grass,
carried her off
as he carries mountains and valleys,
countries and seas.

And this woman would whisper:
the world's my bed.
The world—streams, rivers,
oceans—and me!

Here I am, afloat like a sailor's daughter
and the world's my boat.
A swarm of stars like a swarm of bees
hums around the world.

The world clings to my belly,
my hands sprout like flowers from the ground.
And here on this huge world, delight
comes over my limbs.

A small woman made the world
her bed
—that great big world.
And it wasn't unknown to the world
that a small woman
was resting on him.

DELIGHT

There I knew a delight beyond delight,
and that was the Sabbath day
when all the branches reached up to the light.

Like a bubbling river, the light streamed everywhere,
and the wheel of the eye desired the wheel of the sun.
Then I knew a delight beyond delight.

The treetops blazed, the light couldn't have its fill,
molten in the waves, it set the river on fire,
would have swallowed my head too, like a golden orange.

Water lilies opened their mouths to devour
the river in its hurry, the tall grass floating by.
And that day was the Sabbath day
when all the trees reached up in their desire.
Then I knew a delight beyond delight.

THE LAND OF THE SETTING SUN

> *And he took away the horses*
> *that the kings of Judah had given*
> *to the sun, ... and burned*
> *the chariots of the sun with fire.*

I heard there is a way to the land
of the setting sun,
but nobody ever said it's a land
where I could go.

I had no friend to come with me
so I set out alone
for the land where the setting sun
rides a chariot of gold.

And they told me: kings without equal,
magnificent kings,
ruled over the land of the setting sun
long, long ago.

And I told myself: When I come to the land
of the setting sun,
they'll give me a robe of purple,
a throne of gold.

And in that land I will find peace
for ever and ever.
—That tale I made up myself.
That tale I was never told.

NIGHT SORROW

The way is so long
and the new moon's like hammered tin,
and who can tell gold
from a bit of tin
that's worth a worn penny.

Steaming clouds float in the sky,
roofs and towers rise up in their misery,
and a howling of foxes fills the air,
their backs shiver in the thorn-hedge.

The stars, the planets swarm.
Night drops into the sea of nights
and the light leaps like a deer,
like a spring
gushing from a wall.

Breakers claw at the naked surf and pierce
the terrible depths,
and the sheaves of the field stand up
and the reeds
raise their voices in song:
> *Return O my soul and rest thee*
> *For the Lord has blest thee*

The way is so long
and the new moon's like hammered tin
and above it, whiter than milk, that light
streaming
like salvation.

SOMEONE TO SAVE HIM

There was once a man sick unto death
and his sickness grew worse
and he waited and waited for someone to save him
for he said in his heart: Someone will save me.

And his brother said: Someone will save him.
And his uncle said: Someone will save him.
And they didn't give him another thought
for they said in their hearts: Someone will save him.

So that man kept wasting away,
wasting away from day to day,
but he didn't want to blame his brother
for he said in his heart: Someone will save me.

And he lay on the bed where he would die
and was full of faith: Someone will save me.
All day long he said: Someone will save me.
Who wouldn't want to speak that way?

And his brother said: Yes, someone will save him.
Today or tomorrow someone will save him.
I'm sure that someone will come to save him.
But a stranger cried out: "No one will save him!"

So the sick man kept wasting away
and his refrain was: Someone to save me.
But he didn't want to blame his brother—
how could he ever blame him?

AROUND JERUSALEM

There is a train that goes around
and around Jerusalem
at night.

Birds circle above it,
beat their wings with a great noise,
drop a feather in the dark
onto the threshing-floor
of the Jebusite.

Black trees run along the tracks,
cavern calls out to cave.
A dry ravine lies at its feet
and brilliant gravelstone.

At night there's a train
that goes around
and around Jerusalem.

Mountains circle it,
winds moan at it from the ruins,
birds shriek out of the silence,
owl eyes glimmer.

Mountains hang over it
like a coronet, a crown.
And a great mass grinds the dust, roars
like a hunted lion.

A clattering in the night,
the cauldron
of awful darkness.
That mammoth roars: Hallelujah!

BEHIND THE RAIN

Kislev and Nisan, like yoked horses,
storm around the planet's wheel.
In the moon of Tammuz the wind roars,
flogs the tree with knotted whips.
Lions no longer scold the night,
no angels sing their chants at night.
The wind roars like a seething cauldron.
There's a god hiding behind the rain.

Embers smolder deep in the mountain,
the night is charred like the sides of a pot.
At the new moon you will sweep us away
in a swift, graceful sailing ship
across the face of the Great Sea.
At the new moon, the sea will flood,
and in its cunning the stricken tree
will flower at dawn in a burst of red.
How bitter it is when the wind roars!

In the moon of Tammuz the tree moans
when the wind flogs it with knotted whips.
The moon of Nisan slips away like a thief,
the moon of Kislev, like chaff in the wind.
The wind roars like a seething cauldron.
There's a god hiding behind the rain.

MAGIC

Today I'm a hill,
tomorrow a sea.
Always wandering
like Miriam's well,
always a bubble
lost in the gorges.

Last night I dreamt
red horses, purple,
green—

In the morning I listened:
an endless babbling of water,
a chatter of parrots.

Today I'm a snail,
tomorrow a giant
palm tree.

Yesterday a cave,
today I'm a seashell.
Tomorrow
I'll be tomorrow.

TIME CAUGHT IN A NET

And again I was like one of those little girls,
fingernails black with work,
building tunnels in the sand.

Wherever my eye rested
there were ribbons of purple
and many eyes shining like silver pearls.

Again I was like one of those little girls
who sail around the whole world in one night
till they come to the land of Cathay
and Madagascar,

and who break cups and saucers
from so much love,
so much love,
so much love.

DISTANT LAND

Tonight I came back in a sailing boat
from the isles of the sun, the coral reefs.
Girls with golden combs in their hair
remained on the islands of the sun.

Four slow years of honey and milk
I wandered around on the isles of the sun.
The fruit stands were always laden,
the cherries shone in the sun.

Mariners from seventy lands
were sailing off to the isles of the sun.
I counted the golden ships—
four years in that streaming light.

Four slow years, round as an apple,
I stayed there, stringing coral beads.
In the isles of the sun, merchants and peddlers
spread out their crimson silks.

And the sea was deeper than any depth
when I came back from the isles of the sun.
Heavy as honey, the drops of sun
fell on the island when the sun went down.

HEARTBREAK IN THE PARK

In sunny Hyde Park
facing the warm stone gate,
mothers and grandmas
drifted by without touching me.

Schoolboys who cut class
were pestering the ducks in the water.
A dog exploded into the lake
and the congregation
of ducks ran away, insulted.
The old people rested on the canvas chairs.
And I knew:
whatever's gone for a while might as well be
lost forever.

A smell of vanilla filled the genteel café across the road
where nice husbands
went to get their wives' coats.
A student from the country stretched out on the grass,
looked up at the sky,
fingering the clouds.
A colorful mob flounced up and down the steps,
busses wobbled by
like a herd of red elephants.

All of that broke my heart,
I couldn't say a word.
I knew I could wander around
and no one would stop me.
Not far away was another pond with its boats
and all its twittering and chirping.

A HARD WINTER

DUST

Imagine: only the dust
came along with me,
I had no other companion.
Came with me to kindergarten,
rumpled my hair
on the warmest days.

Imagine who came along with me
and everyone else had another companion.
When winter spreads terrible nets, when the clouds
devour their prey,
imagine who came with me
and how much
I wanted another companion.

The pine cones rustled
and I ached to be alone with the wind.
Nights I dreamed in a fever
about houses wet with love.
Imagine how unfair
that the dust
was my only companion.

On the days of the hot wind, I'd sail away
to the city of the leviathans,
full of a wild delight.
I'd never come back, not as long as I lived.

But when I came back,
I was like a raven despised
by his cousins the ravens.
I had no companion at all,
only the dust
came along with me.

REQUIEM AFTER SEVENTEEN YEARS

The cantor was reading psalms.
The trees whispered
like a flock of black priests.

We weren't much taller than the gravestones
and we knew there would be
no resurrection in our day.

From there the ladder reached up
to the ranks of the holy and pure
who shine like sapphire.
(All of them lay at our feet).

Our lives were like a grasshopper's
on the border of sun and shade.

But when the drowned girl passed through
all the chambers of the sea
we knew

that the sea
is the father of rivers.

I couldn't understand why my heart
was so pinched by the heat.
I thought about the roses, their orange color.
There was nothing more beautiful than the roses.
In the patchy thicket, the heat
hung like a bat.

All of it broke my heart so much, broke
my heart.
Then I melted away
like the buzzing of a wasp as it flies past.

TRYING

Remember you promised to come on the holiday
an hour after dark.
I've left debts in a number of places,
would you care to settle them?
Since you'll be coming after dark
no one will notice you.
Since you'll be coming after dark
I will certainly notice you.

I don't understand why the house
though it's heated, doesn't get warm.
It's as if the walls were flinching with pain
inside the plaster,
yet we keep pushing it all away
from day to day till the end of time.
What a fraud: to act as if we
were the sons of gods.

Remember you promised to come on the holiday
an hour after dark.
I won't keep count of wrongs
till you get here.
And you: don't believe what I say
when it's odd or perverse.
I go to sleep like everyone else,
I don't practice magic.
I forgo the honors in advance,
I'm not the daughter of gods.

Remember when and where.

TRYING AGAIN

If I could only get all of you,
how could I ever get all of you—
even more than beloved icons,
more than a quarried mountainside,
more than mines
of burning coal,
say the mines of extinguished coal
and the breath of day burning like a furnace.

If I could get you for all the years,
how could I ever get you from all the years—
how to stretch out one arm
like a river branching in Africa,
like dreaming the Bay of Storms,
dreaming a ship that went down,
the way you imagine clouds as a bed,
lilies of clouds spread beneath you,
but when you need them they won't support you,
don't believe they'll support you.

If I could get hold of every particle of you,
if I could get hold of you like metal—
say pillars of copper,
a pillar of purple copper (that pillar
I remembered last summer)—
and the bottom of the ocean I've never seen,
the bottom of the ocean I see
under the weight of a thousand layers of air,
a thousand and one held breaths.

If I could only have all of you
as you are now,
how could you ever become
like a part of me.

HERON

Tomorrow I'll come to him early.
Let the meddlers shrivel like bitter apples,
and the ones who think they're so clever,
let them be silenced—
That's what will happen tomorrow,
in the beginning.

That's how I'd like to come to him tomorrow.
My dreams will lose their thorns,
will run over with longings,
won't fade away at the usual hour.

Maybe he'll stand close to me.
I could hover above him like a bird,
I could shine like the eye in the peacock's tail.

That's the one who takes all the prizes,
who has blighted me with love—

Like a bird he'll never be taken.

HILLS OF SALT

Foam fluttered on the sea like birds' wings.
Two salt hills were left on the beach,
and the sea was a country of lakes,
with sailboats small as a thumb
gleaming
like soap bubbles.

The two of us sat there, each by his lakes,
a strip of sand between us
and a mass of seaweed.
The heavy fronds swayed back and forth,
clinging to the pointed rocks in their shrill lust.

A frond of seaweed broke loose and fell at my feet,
and my eyelids were heavy with sun.
And the sea rose up and spilled over
from pool to pool,
blue streams in a net of light.

The sea foamed in the palms of our hands,
the sand between us—two arms wide.
But we didn't draw close all that day,
not by a hairsbreadth,
our bodies two salt hills and our feet
seaweed.

THE RAGING WATERS

A bird twittered like crazy
till it couldn't anymore
and then it wept.
I sank in a cloud of pleasure,
I sank,
I melted away.
No, I was drowned in the ocean,
there a man loved me,
didn't leave me a fingernail.
His hand caught me by the hair,
in the ocean's pounding
I nearly went under.
His hand
dragged me by the hair
in the teeming ocean. I no longer
remember
a thing.

MAHLON AND CHILION

What is this wondrous thing?
If this wonder seizes me
like a viper on a patch of black water,
my day will darken, I'll be lost.

If this wonder seizes me,
I'll be scattered over the seven waters.
Arms and legs, swept by the waters
to that wondrous place.

What is this wondrous thing?
Glints of light in the water, vipers
in the desert
sigh like me, like me.

But what is this wondrous thing?
This wonder has already stricken me,
my head flies away twittering,
I am lost and sing like a fool.

A HARD WINTER

The wick shook in the candle flame,
and before its glory vanished
it was lapped in sadness.

Rain and sun ruled by turns: in the house
we were afraid to think
what would become of us.

The bushes reddened at their hearts
and the pond hid away.
Each of us was sunk in himself alone.

But for a moment, distracted,
I saw
how people are cut off from this world

like trees struck by lightning,
heavy with flesh and sinew,
the wet branches trampled like dead grass.

The shutter was damaged, the walls thin.
Rain and sun, by turns, rode over us
with iron wheels.

All the plants were intent
on themselves alone.
This time I never thought I'd survive.

ABUSE

In that place,
one of those places,
the flowers were gnawed to shreds,
devoured like prey,
dogs bared their teeth,
barked in their fury—
the flowers were gnawed to shreds.
My God,
was there beauty!

In that place,
different from all those places,
they were like sunflowers
trailing the sun—
when they lifted their heads
their fragrance followed the sun.
And hours after they were torn apart,
even after they died,
that soul still burned in them.
My God,
was there abuse!

THEY TOLD ME TO BRING

They told me to bring flowers of every color
and whatever time carried off,
and a night when the moon is whole
as a new undamaged coin
from the Emperor's mint.
And our hearts rejoiced that the coin
was not defiled.

They told me to bring unworked clay,
the love of the Philistine princes,
a Dagon cut down in front of their door,
an infant who died on the palms of Beelzebub,
and those who've gone down into the dust
and send up a glimmer from among the dead.

They told me to bring whatever I could,
the leftover plunder
from all the underworlds.

A GREAT TREMOR

When the bells tolled, when the muezzin wailed
and the rooster protested against the moon,
a great tremor seized Jerusalem
and the King's palace
lit up the streets.

In Solomon's stables
monkeys and parrots shrieked,
the ones Queen Tahpenes sent him
by merchants and highwaymen.

The still waters of Shiloah gathered to a cataract,
roaring into the Valley of Hinnom,
shattering
in the clefts of rock.

In Solomon's stables,
princes would serve for a daily wage
until the King wished to harness his chariot.

When the bells tolled, when the muezzin wailed,
two border guards took to bed,
cursing.
On a cloud black as a Negro's hand,
Jerusalem the City of David was hurled away
like a finger torn from the body.

THE BLUE WEST

If there was nothing but a road there,
the ruins of some workshops,
one fallen minaret
and a few carcasses of machines,
why couldn't I
come to the heart of the field?
There is nothing more painful
than a field
with a stone on its heart.

I want to reach the other side of the hill,
want to reach—
want to be there.
I want to break out of the mass of the earth,
from my head to the bottom of my feet—
the mass of the earth.

I want to reach the ends of thought
whose beginnings
slice like a knife.
I want to climb up to the fringes of the sun
and not be eaten by fire.

If only we could walk about
with grasshopper feet on the water,
if only we could climb
on a high arch of the sun's rays,

If only we could reach
all the cities beyond the sea—
And I'll tell you another sorrow:
a seashore where there are no ships.

On one of the days to come
the eye of the sea will grow dark
from all the many ships.
In that hour, the mass of the earth
will be spread as a cloth.

And a sun will shine for us blue as the sea,
a sun will shine for us warm as an eye,
will wait until we climb up
as it heads for the blue west.

THE THIRD BOOK

SURELY YOU REMEMBER

After they all leave,
I remain alone with the poems,
some poems of mine, some of others.
I prefer poems that others have written.
I remain quiet, and slowly
the knot in my throat dissolves.
I remain.

Sometimes I wish everyone would go away.
Maybe it's nice, after all, to write poems.
You sit in your room and the walls grow taller.
Colors deepen.
A blue kerchief becomes a deep well.

You wish everyone would go away.
You don't know what's the matter with you.
Perhaps you'll think of something.
Then it all passes, and you are pure crystal.

After that, love.
Narcissus was so much in love with himself.
Only a fool doesn't understand
he loved the river, too.

You sit alone.
Your heart aches, but
it won't break.
The faded images wash away one by one.
Then the defects.
A sun sets at midnight. You remember
the dark flowers too.

You wish you were dead or alive or
somebody else.
Isn't there a country you love? A word?
Surely you remember.

Only a fool lets the sun set when it likes.
It always drifts off too early
westward to the islands.

Sun and moon, winter and summer
will come to you,
infinite treasures.

TWO SONGS OF THE GARDEN

1

Some ants found half a dead fly
and it wasn't easy for them
to drag it off the grass.
Their little sides nearly burst with the effort.
And at that very moment, the grass
bristled suddenly, like a field of barley.
What madness, that the grass
should consider itself a field of barley.
I knew the ants' fate would be bitter:
all that hard labor, and an early death.
A few well-fed insects poked about in the grass
and the foolish ants had to hear their droning.
Every one of the flowers bloomed
as well as it could,
the roses more showy than last year.
Then I cried.
Beside me, all of them had become
such giants.

2

A swarm of gnats seethes every day at six.
My poor grass grows hunchback.
Every day I want to ask for something.
The sun no longer seems like a ball of fire,
it's seething inside.
No air to breathe, there is only
pleading.
I tell you, if this summer passes,
everything will be restored:
the flower to the plant, the wing
to the bird.
The sand that wandered off will return to the bay.
With a few stalks of corn and some leaves
stricken by aphids
it's impossible to live.
I tell you it's impossible to live.

So many things growing
and hardly a one of them
in bloom.

AUSTRALIA

At the southern end of the world, Australia—
island of summer rain,
less than one inhabitant
per square kilometer.

What do the Australians do
on their cold June nights,
their warm Christmas,
the monsoon rains?

At the southern end of the world, Australia,
an unpopulated continent,
farther away than Malaya,
farther than Singapore.

On the map, Australia
floats along in the ocean
as if it weren't very far
from the South Pole.

How idyllic, you might have thought:
sheep-shearing in Australia.
The gold-miners came there,
the white settlers.
Lonely,
without women,
they wasted their days in Australia.

How far away Australia is!
Only the kangaroo hops around there—
that human animal,
carrying her young on her belly.

At the southern end of the garden,
where the sprinkler doesn't reach,
it's like Australia. Arid.
Stunted shrubbery, swarms
of nomadic ants, wild bees.
Dry soil
and the grass has a hard time growing.
Only weeds grow wild there
as in the bush—
wild men dancing around the fire.

NOW THE MOON

Now the moon
gets thinner and fades,
goes bad, withers,
grows hoarse and sets.

And yet
maybe the rainclouds
are puffing up its belly,
it seems to be swelling.
A thin veil is spread out over the sky.
The moon gets thinner and sets
as if it were lopped off,
falling.
These soft clouds have made it rot.

But wait—
behind it a pale circle
is already rising:
the full moon of last month
shining again.

Light as a seed between
webs of sky
or fat as a gourd.
Now it's the waning moon,
now the ripe moon about to drop.
Look at it, love: it always
comes back.

VANILLA

She sits in the house for days on end.
She reads the papers.
(Come on now, don't you?)
She doesn't do what she'd like to do,
things get in the way.
She wants vanilla, lots of vanilla,
give her vanilla.

In winter she's cold, really cold,
colder than other people.
She bundles up but she's still cold.
She wants vanilla.

She wasn't born yesterday, if that's
what you're thinking.
It's not the first time she's felt the cold.
Not the first time it's winter.
In fact summer isn't so pleasant either.
She reads the papers more than she'd like to.
In winter she won't budge without the heater.
Sometimes she gets sick of it all.
Did she ever ask you for much?
You've got to admit she hasn't.
She wants vanilla.

Take a close look: she's wearing
a plaid skirt.
She likes plaid because it's cheerful.
Just to look at her, you'd laugh.
It's all so ridiculous,
even she laughs about it sometimes.
She has a hard time in winter,
a rough time in summer,
you'd laugh.

You could call her mimosa, a bird
that won't fly,
you could call her plenty of things.
She's always bundling up in something or other
till she's choking.
Why bundle up if you could choke?
These things are complicated.
It's the cold in winter, the exaggerated
heat in summer,
never the way you want it.

And by the way, don't forget,
she wants vanilla.
Now she's even crying.
Give her vanilla.

THE MARIONETTE

To be a marionette.
In the precious gray light before dawn
to pass beneath the new day,
deep in the undercurrents.
To be a marionette,
a pale slender doll of porcelain,
held by threads.

To be a marionette.
The threads that bind my whole life
are pure silk.
A marionette—
she too is real.
She has memories.

Four hundred years ago
she was Doña Elvira, Contessa of Seville,
with three hundred chambermaids.
The moment she glanced at her fine
silk handkerchief,
she knew her fate: she'd be a wax doll
or a porcelain marionette.

Doña Elvira, Contessa of Seville, would dream
of late-ripening vines.
Her courtiers always spoke softly to her.
Doña Elvira, the Contessa et cetera,
was gathered unto her people.
She left two sons and a daughter
to a gloomy future.

In the twentieth century, on a precious gray dawn,
how fortunate to be
a marionette.
This woman is not responsible for her actions,
say the judges.
Her fragile heart is gray as dawn,
her body hangs
by a thread.

PURE MEMORY

Only when the face is blotted out
can you remember anything fully,
only when the face
is blotted out.

First the lights go wild,
the colors start from their frames.
Stars plunge from their height like epileptics.
Grasses moan,
the new growth more painful
than wilting.

Whatever blinds our eyes
retreats to the shadows.
And the face, too.
Something stirs in the depths.

How many days, years,
thunderstorms
have we waited for one
pure memory
to break from the depths of the earth
bright red as a poppy.

IMAGINATION IS A BOUNDLESS THING

The everlasting forests won't last forever
if lightning strikes them—
from distant lands come rumors
about an earthquake.
The vision of the Yellow River no longer leads me astray
for there's nothing in it but water
and that goes down in the end to one of the seas.

Imagination is a boundless thing
but when you're thinking clearly,
how is the Black Sea different from the Caspian Sea?
A man of thirty is not like a child:
he stops hoping for miracles, won't be seduced
by the heart's noise.
He doesn't lose his head, not even after sunset
when the marvelous sea darkens and hides its sharks.

But the rumors keep returning: a rumor is something
that can't be stopped.
Rumor drives rumor around the world
as the wind drives the waves.
First the rumors bear you up like Ophelia,
then they sweep you away into the depths
and all the dreams of your youth, all your imagination
won't pull you out of the waters.

THE HORNS OF HITTIN

In the morning strange ships appeared on the sea,
prow and stern
in the ancient fashion.
In the eleventh century
columns of crusader ships sailed off,
kings and rabble.
Crates of gold and plunder lay around in the ports,
ships of gold,
piers of gold.
The sun lit marvelous flames in them,
burning forests.
When the sun dazzled and the waves rocked,
their hearts went out to Byzantium.
How cruel and naive the crusaders were.
They plundered everything.

A boundless terror seized the villagers.
Their daughters were carried off,
blue-eyed grandsons were born to them
in shame.
No one spared their honor.

Slender-necked ships set sail for Egypt.
The magnificent troops marched on Acre,
a lightning force.
Each man a swift knight bearing
the Bishop's blessing. A great flock
of wolves.

How their blue eyes lit up
when they saw the palm trees sway in the wind.
How they soiled their beards with spittle
when they dragged women into the brush.

They built many fortresses,
snipers' towers, ramparts of basalt.
How their bastards in the villages
marvelled at them.

In the twelfth century, the Marquis of Montfort
began to fail.
The winds of Galilee whistled over his gloomy fortress.
A curving scimitar burst from the East
like a jester's staff.
Saladin advanced from the East in gaudy colors.
With the horns of a wild beast
he gored them hip and thigh, that infidel dog:
Saladin
did them in
at the Horns of Hittin.

No kingdom remained to them,
no life eternal,
no Jerusalem.
How cruel and naive the crusaders were.
They plundered everything.

PRIDE

I tell you, even rocks crack,
and not because of age.
For years they lie on their backs
in the heat and the cold,
so many years,
it almost seems peaceful.
They don't move, so the cracks stay hidden.
A kind of pride.
Years pass over them, waiting there.
Whoever is going to shatter them
hasn't come yet.
And so the moss flourishes, the seaweed
whips around,
the sea pushes through and rolls back—
the rocks seem motionless.
Till a little seal comes to rub against them,
comes and goes away.
And suddenly the rock has an open wound.
I told you, when rocks break, it happens by surprise.
And people, too.

A DRESS OF FIRE

You know, she said, they made you
a dress of fire.
Remember how Jason's wife burned in her dress?
It was Medea, she said, Medea did that to her.
You've got to be careful, she said,
they made you a dress that glows
like an ember, that burns like coals.

Are you going to wear it, she said, don't wear it.
It's not the wind whistling, it's the poison
seeping in.
You're not even a princess, what can you do to Medea?
Can't you tell one sound from another, she said,
it's not the wind whistling.

Remember, I told her, that time when I was six?
They shampooed my hair and I went out into the street.
The smell of shampoo trailed after me like a cloud.
Then I got sick from the wind and the rain.
I didn't know a thing about reading Greek tragedies,
but the smell of the perfume spread
and I was very sick.
Now I can see it's an unnatural perfume.

What will happen to you now, she said,
they made you a burning dress.
They made me a burning dress, I said. I know.
So why are you standing there, she said,
you've got to be careful.
You know what a burning dress is, don't you?

I know, I said, but I don't know
how to be careful.
The smell of that perfume confuses me.
I said to her, No one has to agree with me,
I don't believe in Greek tragedies.

But the dress, she said, the dress is on fire.
What are you saying, I shouted,
what are you saying?
I'm not wearing a dress at all,
what's burning is me.

A PERSONAL OPINION

Pain has no use,
I assure you:
a worm in a piece of fruit
won't make the fruit taste better.
I know you,
I can see what your childhood did to you,
how your face grows sour.
That's not the way heroes are made.

Heroes are different, it seems to me,
they're not milkweed.
They fight in the air, on the sea, even in Manchuria,
always some strange faraway place.
How my heart goes out to them: to the air, to the sea,
even to Manchuria—
but let them not dream of medals.
I'm sorry to say they die like dogs.
As a rule they're used for stoking up locomotives,
as in Manchuria.

Pain is inhuman,
I insist,
there are no extenuating circumstances.
Look, isn't it monstrous:
someone secretly dying away,
growing blacker and blacker,
withering,
without a wife, without sons.

IN CHAD AND CAMEROON

By the waters of Chad and Cameroon
Europeans are waiting, sick of life.
They no longer care about manners.

Not far from them
a group of lepers passes by.
Old men without fingers.

When evening comes, the wind
doesn't stir.
It's as hot as it was.

Only a reddish glow rises from the waters
in Chad and Cameroon
and falls on the Europeans.

HOW HONG KONG WAS DESTROYED

I am in Hong Kong.
There's a tongue of a river here swarming
with snakes.
There are Greeks, Chinese, Negroes.
Near the paper lanterns, carnival crocodiles
open their jaws wide.
Who said they eat you alive here?
A huge crowd went down to the river.
You've never seen such silk in your life,
redder than poppy blossoms.

In Hong Kong
the sun rises in the East
and they water the flowers with a perfumed spray
to double their scent.
But the evening wind batters the paper lanterns,
and if someone's murdered, they ask,
Was it a Chinaman? a Negro?
Did he die in pain?
Then they pitch his body into the river
and all the reptiles feed.

I am in Hong Kong.
In the evening the café lights dimmed
and paper lanterns ripped in the streets.
The ground seethed and exploded
seethed and exploded
and I alone knew
there is nothing in the West
and nothing in the East.

The paper dragon yawned
but the ground exploded.
Enemies will come here
who've never seen silk in their lives.

Only the little prostitutes
dressed in soiled silk
still receive their guests
in tiny alcoves filled with lanterns.
In the morning they weep
for their rotting flesh.
And if someone's killed, they ask,
Chinaman? Negro? Poor thing,
let's hope he didn't die in pain.
And already at dusk the first
visitors arrive
like a thorn in the living flesh.

I am in Hong Kong
and Hong Kong hangs on the ocean,
a colored lantern on a hook
at the end of the world.
Perhaps the dragon
will swathe it in crimson silk
and let it drop
into the abyss of the stars.
And only the little prostitutes will sob into the silk.
Even now,
still now,
men pinch them in the belly.

I am not in Hong Kong
and Hong Kong is not in the world.
Where Hong Kong used to be
there's a reddish stain
half in the water and half in the sky.

IN THE RIGHT WIND

When a man sits alone in his room
what do people outside know about him?
There may be something buzzing in his ears
twenty-four hours a day.
Some people just don't understand how difficult
the day is for him.
Morning doesn't shine as it ought to,
the sun's like a flattened disk,
and some people don't even know
how ugly
a flattened disk can be.

Twenty-five years ago
there was a terrible war in the world.
In a thousand falling houses were men and women,
their hearts in flood.
The man who sits alone in his room
looks at the flattened sun.
He begins to think about marvelous things,
like flying
in the right wind.

There are those who can fly without even needing
the right wind.
Pine branches catch at their cheeks, they fly
with moist open lips.

Suddenly the dust of a cloud or a floating seed
touches them on the mouth
without their knowing it.
They cry when they see
the sky's amazing blue.
When some heavenly body brushes against them,
it does them no harm.

Flying means that the layers of air carry you
as if in love.
You take off, you land.
And this may surprise you:
some people fly in the right wind
and die, suddenly, before their time.

THE END OF THE FALL

If a man falls from a plane in the middle of the night
God alone can raise him.
God appears at his side in the middle of the night,
touches the man and relieves
his suffering.
God doesn't wipe away his blood
for blood is not the soul,
God doesn't comfort his body
for the man is not flesh.
God bends over him, lifts up his head
and gazes at him.
In God's eyes the man is a small child.
He gets up clumsily on all fours and wants to walk,
then feels he has wings.
The man is still confused: he doesn't know
it's easier to glide than to crawl.
God would like to stroke his head
but hesitates.
He doesn't want to alarm the man
with signs of love.

If a man falls from a plane in the middle of the night
God alone knows where the fall ends.

EVEN A THOUSAND YEARS

I can't remake the world
and there's no sense in it either.
Day unto day and day unto night declare nothing.
In the spring, sweet-peas, lilacs and roses come up,
everything life-size and in natural color.
Nothing really new grows here,
not once in ten years.

Whoever wants to breathe attar of roses,
let him gather it from the wind,
and whoever wants to plant a tree,
let him plant a fig tree—
he'll never get to enjoy it himself.

You ask if I've ever seen beauty?
Well, I've seen quite a bit,
but not in the right places.
Say, that waterfall:
of course I've seen it, what then?
A thundering waterfall isn't such a pretty sight.
Beauty doesn't walk around in the open air,
sometimes it's inside a room
when the doors are locked and the shutters down.
Really, the most beautiful things
aren't rivers or shores or mountains.
I know too much about all of that
to fool myself.

After the pain there's just curiosity
to see what happens in the end
to everything beautiful.

Of course I don't have to plant a fig tree.
I can always wait for spring,
the roses, the hyacinths.

But in time people grow tough
as fingernails,
gray, stubborn as stone.
Perhaps it's an attractive prospect
to turn into a block of salt
with a mineral strength.
To stare empty-eyed
at this potash and phosphate factory
even a thousand years.

DEEP CALLETH UNTO DEEP

DAY UNTO DAY UTTERETH SPEECH

As in the forests on Mount Carmel
where my soul was filled with yearning—
the pines dropped their needles
when the wind rose,
pine cones fell to the ground.

My house was drawn closed with draperies
I sewed of Chinese silk,
but the light came through,
light flooded the sills.

We spent our lives without even noticing,
I lost track of the years.
King David came to me
after he returned from the dead.
He'd sit beside me day after day,
when he was pleased he'd play hymns:
The heavens declare the glory of God.

As in the forests of Carmel,
pine cones were falling, falling endlessly.

MIDNIGHT SONG

Once again, as in years past,
the bedroom's upside down,
ashes everywhere,
clothes dropped in a heap,
a pile of unanswered letters
and one warm bed.
Besides, there's a flu epidemic
and here I am again, if you please,
flat on my back.

This year
and all the years to come,
I won't give up one little bird
that flies around in my garden,
won't exchange one little bird
for a cardinal or a dove.

Another year will come—
once again, as always,
my throat's choked with love.

POEM OF EXPLANATIONS

Some people know now to love,
for others it's just not right.
Some people kiss in the street,
others find it unpleasant
—and not only in the street.

I think it's a talent like any other,
perhaps that's an advantage.
Like the rose of Sharon with its gift for blooming,
like the lily of the valley
that chooses its colors.
A rose or a lily in bloom
is blinding.
I don't mean to offend: I know
there are other kinds.

Hummingbirds are the loveliest of birds
in my opinion,
but if you like, you can go to the sparrow.

Even so, I keep telling myself,
I'm not a bird of paradise,
I'm not a three-headed calf,
I'm not an apple that doesn't ripen.

SAND

Then we walked down to the beach again
and again I said what's going to happen
and he said it's too soon to talk,
what a pity, but things may change.
And again I said that so many times,
so many times he says to me
or keeps trying
to talk about anything but.

And again we held each other for a while
and even looked for a nicer spot.
When it got late we shook out our clothes
and again I hinted that shouldn't we think,
again I said it's like the sand,
what he answered slips my mind.
And there, yes,
by the sea,
everything slipped through my fingers like sand.

DEEP CALLETH UNTO DEEP

In Jerusalem I had my days of roses.
(What is Jerusalem but a hive of old houses?)
I came there young and returned, years later,
strange even to myself.
Alone, in a house that wasn't mine,
I lifted my eyes to the hills
to see if help had come.

Clouds lashed at each other,
dark cypresses rustled beneath me—
Suddenly a weird flash of sun
swooped down
from the ends of the West.

And my longings flooded me,
sawed in my head like a cricket,
swarmed like hornets—

I was that drunk.

IN JERUSALEM

Of all things, at the funeral.
(The sun was cruel even in winter.)
I saw the slopes of Ein Karem,
the monastery and the orchards,
hills below hills,
hills beyond hills,
and in the brush
a monastery roof or two.

I know where he lives but not
where to find him.
Mostly he's not to be found,
like Jerusalem
hidden by a cloud.

I want to be with him
in light or in darkness
—and in Jerusalem, too.
Do I have to say he's good-looking?
How easily I praise him.

Of all things, at the funeral,
as it moved from Ein Karem to the cemetery
with so many cars,
so many mourners,
I felt suddenly content.
I wanted to live
—perhaps in Jerusalem.

But even that's more than I meant.
I wanted him.

LIKE RACHEL

To die like Rachel
when the soul shivers like a bird,
wants to escape.
Behind the tent, Jacob and Joseph
speak about her, trembling.
Her life turns head over heels inside her
like that infant
ready to be born.

How hard it is.
Jacob's love ate away at her
greedily.
Now she's dying,
she has no use for any of that.

Suddenly the infant's cry—
Jacob comes into the tent, but Rachel
doesn't even notice him.
Pleasure bathes her face,
washes over her head.

A great ease descends on her.
Her breath won't stir a feather now.
They laid her to rest among mountain stones
and did not mourn her.

To die
like Rachel.

KING OVER ISRAEL

Always in the back seat of the car,
the sky arid as a field of thorns,
no resting place for my eyes
from one end of the sky to the other.

White nights
are terrible as the face of a beast
baring its teeth at a desert bush.
But nights black as chimney soot
were no better in my eyes.

This Dead Sea has no water for the thirsty,
my eyes find no resting place in the course of the stars.
So many years in the back seat
like a field passed over by the rain.

This field has no water for the thirsty.

The man who walked in the streets of Jerusalem,
a crown of thorns to mock him,
knew the taste of a field
with no sign of water for the thirsty.

The man who walked up the streets of Jerusalem,
torments weighing on his heart,
saw his end before him always
when he saw the sky
arid as a field of thorns.

And I, in the back seat,
so many years in the back seat,

I, too, learned not to trust
ships that appear to be sailing on the sea.

I, Koheleth, was king over Israel in Jerusalem.

How the city sat solitary.

IMPOVERISHMENT

If I must be impoverished
let it be like an arid land,
if I must
let it be with pride.
You have to save Torah scrolls from the fire
but don't save me.
My wish is
to be like some wrecked ship
when I die.
Waters without end
will drown the flame.

FROM DAY TO NIGHT

Every day I wake up again
as if for the last time.
I don't know what's waiting for me,
perhaps that's a sign
nothing is waiting for me.

The coming spring
is like the one that's gone.
I know what the month of April means
but to me it means nothing.
I can't tell the boundary that divides
day from night.
Night is colder,
but both are equally silent.

At dawn I hear the sound of birds
and fall asleep easily
out of affection for them.
The one I love isn't here,
perhaps he
isn't anywhere.

I pass from day to day
from day to night
like a feather the bird doesn't feel
when it drops.

THE SOUND OF BIRDS AT NOON

This chirping
is not in the least malicious.
They sing without giving us a thought
and they are as many
as the seed of Abraham.
They have a life of their own,
they fly without thinking.
Some are rare, some common,
but every wing is grace.
Their hearts aren't heavy
even when they peck at a worm.
Perhaps they're light-headed.
The heavens were given to them
to rule over day and night
and when they touch a branch,
the branch too is theirs.
This chirping is entirely free of malice.
Over the years
it even seems to have
a note of compassion.

REAL LOVE

IDDO WAKES UP

Iddo
gets up with a trumpet call:
suddenly he's awake.
Little lion,
his sleep ran away.

One minute and he bursts out crying.
Doesn't mean to annoy.
His sleep ran away.

He holds out both hands:
issues a request.
Sends for water,
some porridge to eat,
gulps down a crumb, chases away
the blanket.
Gets good and angry. Sleep
is far away now.

Dear child,
what do you want?
Not much: that everything be done
according to his will.

Suddenly he laughs,
remembers a funny dream,
a tickle in the ribs.
Nice baby.
And what is he trying to do, after all?
shatter rocks?
overturn mountains?

Nice little boy,
he breaks a pan or a spoon
whenever the spirit moves him.
My love in the morning,
the evening,
the whole day long.

THE GLASS PAVILION

Lemon tea
at the river. Lunch—
a sandwich and a piece of cake.
I could really see you there,
all the walls were transparent glass.

I could say, Iddo, look!
Look how the ducks in the water
are coming closer!
Look at London, the heart of the city,
look at that squirrel coming down from a tree,
see the new baby grass,
look at the swans somersaulting in the water,
a white one, a black.
The squirrel won't budge. Because of him
you're afraid to pass by.
Look over there: a dark red tree
and a greenish tree with a fat trunk,
scaly and hard,
with a huge head of leaves.
Iddo, look,
Iddo, see:
the entire pavilion is made of glass.

LITTLE CHILD'S HEAD ON THE PILLOW

Things like that don't hurt me anymore—
not what's said in meanness, or stupidity,
or the ordinary mixture
that has something of both.

The choppy surface of the water grows calm.
No wind in the swamp of reeds.
A little child's head rests here on the pillow.
Deep in concentration, I look at it.
What passes between us, one head to the other,
before his eyelids close,
in the warmth of his face, in a glance—
I do not want to say aloud.

THE BEGINNING OF SILENCE

I am waiting for the silence,
waiting for the silence to come.
It's beginning to swarm in the corners.
Now it's about to pounce
like a storm.
It has just touched the red scarf,
the edge of the table,
it's getting closer.
Rainbow tissues in a box,
the odd-colored chairs
here and there around the table.

Now the silence is descending, a huge hand,
wrapping the room in a linen cloth,
wrapping the land, the sea.
It all started with the red scarf
beside the green chair
with a towel spread over it.

And the silence shrieks in me
and I shriek in it.
When I look up, I see worlds
opening, revolving in the room,
in the wide beam of light
cast by the lamp.
And I am quiet. I am calm.

CINDERELLA IN THE KITCHEN

Cinderella spent her best hours
down there in the kitchen.
Her mind was at liberty,
if you want to call it that.
She pressed her hands to her temples,
her hair was splattered with grease.
She set sail in her mind for incomprehensible
distances,
feelings she knew without calling them by name.

She lowered her eyes to her apron,
all spotted and soiled,
and knew what a great distance there is
between here and there,
if one could ever know such a thing.
She knew: whatever begins right now
has no end in time,
no point in time.

She drew a circle around herself,
made a sign for herself,
all in her mind, of course.
She saw those two going out in their finest clothing,
elegant, glittering, dripping perfume,
their necks outstretched.
She didn't really want to be in their place.
Her imagination was filled with treasures—
infinite,
unformed.

She had a little clove of fire in her throat
and a pounding sickly heartbeat.
She was apart from all the others,

weepy, feverish,
ready at any moment
to stop living.

Her lookout was unusually remote,
as if she were on Mars, the planet of war.
She clenched her fists and said:
I'm going out to war!

And then she fell asleep.

THE FINISH LINE

No, it's still not
the finish line.
He's missing a few necessary words,
has lost the thread.
A lack of clarity,
that's his problem, a lack
of clarity.

He lifts his eyes to the window:
shining clouds,
perfectly white,
float across from him
in a distilled sky-blue.

That's a blow for him.
He gets restless.
Of course he should blame himself.
He can't get to the clarity he needs.

A single feather
floats above him in the sky,
falls slowly,
flutters again in the wind
with remarkable precision.
It isn't accustomed to hurrying.
At the dinner table
he'll look for consolation
in a fresh yogurt and a spoonful of jam.

No, he has no reason to respect himself.
Let him study the newspaper instead.
Today won't be the day he'll arrive
at the finish line.

A DECLARATION FOR THE FUTURE

When a man is hungry
or unsure of himself
he makes compromises,
does things he never dreamt of in his life.

Suddenly he's got a crooked back
—what ever happened to his back
that it got so crooked?
Lost pride.
His smile is frozen
and both hands filthy
(so it seems to him)
from touching moist objects
he can't manage to avoid.

He has no choice
(or so it seems):
he'll restrain himself for years,
it's amazing how many years,
and only write down inside himself
day after day
the story of his life.

ROUGH DRAFT

Not to leave footprints,
not to scatter signs,
I'm not going to stay in this place anyway.
Not to write letters,
not to put away souvenirs, photos,
not to arrange them in groups of three in an album.
Not to collect documents,
not to gather in summer,
not to paint or renovate
or settle down.
In the dark to withdraw from the moving caravan,
perhaps after a severe illness
like Rachel.
This business has no dignity,
no importance:
dust on the road, rising
to the sky.
I do not have to arrive.

REQUIEM

He's dead and buried.
Dead and buried, that's that.
No doubt he's dead now.

I had a thing with him once,
nothing really,
just something that happened.
His eyes were like glass, his back
crooked—
even without me he had his troubles.

I came to him on a Saturday,
what Saturday?
a boiling hot Saturday.
Jasmine in bloom,
marigolds,
you name it, my friend,
blooming there in the garden.
(It wasn't his garden.)
He had a roommate,
didn't own a thing.
Flat broke, on top of it all.

So I came that Saturday afternoon,
everything was set
for the chiming of the spheres.
I said I was on my way,
I couldn't stick around,
anyway, I had some other place to go.

He got desperate, didn't try
to hide it.
Said, What'll I do now?

Let him do whatever he wants, I thought.
Anyway, what did I do to him?

Later on, I saw what I did.
When my lover walked out—
that was the worst thing that ever
happened to me.
All of that later.
Meanwhile, he got married, had children,
put down roots.
The years passed over all of us, flying low,
people were shot in the head, the back.
He wasn't hit.

Now he's dead and buried,
dug under and
covered up,
and there's no end but that end.

GADI IN RICHMOND

On the wooden bench in the garden he told me:
I'm afraid to die, even when I get old.
I don't know what it will be like.
How can I know?

It won't be so bad, I told him,
you might even die in your sleep.
Then the Coca Cola spilled
and he laughed and laughed,
he couldn't stop.
He slapped me on the back, really hard,
like a man who's bursting with vigor.

Then he ran over to the deserted pier
and stood there bravely to be photographed
with the geese.
He climbed down the short ladder to the water—
I almost stopped breathing.

The water turned gray under a layer of clouds,
and green near the willow branches.
Later, night made the water grow black,
and the sky, and the river.

A squadron of low-flying planes passed over us,
all of them heading west.

The round globe of the world, calm and clumsy,
also rolled westward.
Then the Coke spilled on his clothes too,
and Gadi
began to laugh again.

BLOOD HEIFER

> *If one be found slain, lying in the field, and it be not known who hath slain him, the elders of the nearest city shall take an heifer, and shall strike off the heifer's neck. And all the elders shall wash their hands over the heifer and say, Our hands have not shed this blood. And the blood shall be forgiven them.*

He took one step,
then a few steps more.
His glasses fell to the ground,
his skullcap.
Managed another step,
bloody, dragging his feet.
Ten steps
and he's not a Jew anymore,
not an Arab—
in limbo.

Havoc in the marketplace; people shouting, Why
are you murdering us?
Others rushing
to take revenge.

And he lies on the ground: a death rattle,
a body torn open,
blood streaming out of the flesh,
streaming
out of the flesh.

He died here, or there—
no one knows for sure.
What do we know?
A dead body lying in the field.

Suffering cleanseth from sin, it is said,
man is like dust in the wind,
but who was that man
lying there lonely in his blood?
What did he see,
what did he hear
with all that commotion around him?
If thou seest even thine enemy's ass
lying under its burden,
it is said, thou shalt surely help.

If a dead body is found lying in the field
if a body is found in the open,
let your elders go out and slaughter a heifer
and scatter its ashes in the river.

YOU CAN'T KILL A BABY TWICE

By the sewage puddles of Sabra and Shatila,
there you transported human beings
in impressive quantities
from the world of the living to the world
of eternal light.

Night after night.
First they shot,
they hanged,
then they slaughtered with their knives.
Terrified women climbed up
on a ramp of earth, frantic:
"They're slaughtering us there,
in Shatila."

A thin crust of moon
over the camps.
Our soldiers lit up the place with searchlights
till it was bright as day.
"Back to the camp,
beat it!" a soldier yelled at
the screaming women from Sabra and Shatila.
He was following orders.
And the children already lying in puddles of filth,
their mouths gaping,
at peace.
No one will harm them.
You can't kill a baby twice.

And the moon grew fuller and fuller
till it became a round loaf of gold.

Our sweet soldiers
wanted nothing for themselves.
All they ever asked
was to come home
safe.

ON THE ATTITUDE TOWARD CHILDREN IN WARTIME

He who destroys thirty children,
it's as if he had destroyed three hundred,
and infants too,
and eight-and-a-half year olds.
(In a year, God willing, they'll be soldiers
in the Palestine Liberation Army.)

Ignorant children, they don't even have
a real world view.
And anyway, their future is shrouded:
refugee shacks, unwashed faces,
open sewers in the streets,
infected eyes.
A negative outlook on life.

And then begins the flight from city to village,
from village to burrows in the hills.
As when a man runs away from a lion,
as when a man runs away from a bear,
from a cannon, from an airplane, runs away
from our troops.

He who destroys thirty children,
it's as if he had destroyed one thousand and thirty,
or one thousand and seventy,
thousand upon thousand.
And because of that, he shall find
no rest.

HOVERING AT A LOW ALTITUDE

I am not here.
I am on those craggy eastern hills
streaked with ice,
where grass doesn't grow
and a wide shadow lies over the slope.
A shepherd girl appears
from an invisible tent,
leading a herd of black goats to pasture.
She won't live out the day,
that girl.

I am not here.
From the deep mountain gorge
a red globe floats up,
not yet a sun.
A patch of frost, reddish, inflamed,
flickers inside the gorge.

The girl gets up early to go to the pasture.
She doesn't walk with neck outstretched
and wanton glances.
She doesn't ask, Whence cometh my help.

I am not here.
I've been in the mountains many days now.
The light will not burn me, the frost
won't touch me.
Why be astonished now?
I've seen worse things in my life.

I gather my skirt and hover
very close to the ground.
What is she thinking, that girl?

Wild to look at, unwashed.
For a moment she crouches down,
her cheeks flushed,
frostbite on the back of her hands.
She seems distracted, but no,
she's alert.

She still has a few hours left.
But that's not what I'm thinking about.
My thoughts cushion me gently, comfortably.
I've found a very simple method,
not with my feet on the ground, and not flying—
hovering
at a low altitude.

Then at noon,
many hours after sunrise,
that man goes up the mountain.
He looks innocent enough.

The girl is right there,
no one else around.
And if she runs for cover, or cries out—
there's no place to hide in the mountains.

I am not here.
I'm above those jagged mountain ranges
in the farthest reaches of the east.
No need to elaborate.
With one strong push I can hover and whirl around
with the speed of the wind.
I can get away and say to myself:
I haven't seen a thing.
And the girl, her palate is dry as a potsherd,
her eyes bulge,
when that hand closes over her hair, grasping it
without a shred of pity.

NEW ZEALAND

No point in going to Africa now.
Plagues, famine, the human body can't take it.
Brutality. They flog people with bullwhips.
Asia—it would make your hair stand on end.
Trapped in the mountains, trapped in the swamps.
The human body can't take it,
who's got the strength?

As for me,
He maketh me to lie down in green pastures
in New Zealand.

Sheep with soft wool, softer
than any wool,
graze there in the meadow.

Truehearted people herd sheep there,
on Sundays they go to church
in their quiet clothes.

No point in hiding it any longer:
we're an experiment that didn't turn out well,
a plan that went wrong,
tied up with too much murderousness.
What do I care about these people,
or those—
screaming till their throats are hoarse,
splitting fine hairs.
Anyway, too much murderousness.

I'm not going to Africa
and not to Asia, either.
I'm not going anywhere.

In New Zealand
in green pastures, beside the still waters,
generous people
will share their bread with me.

IT WILL CERTAINLY COME

Years pass over me here in a stupor,
absent-minded,
dissembling,
waiting for that head to break through
on the horizon,
red as a setting sun.
It will certainly come.
In the entire desert,
hundreds of miles in every direction,
nothing at all resembles it.

I have endless powers of restraint,
I sleep a lot,
wait a lot.
When it comes, everyone will see it.

Sometimes I disguise myself as a dead woman.
When you behave strangely
the neighbors are critical,
whisper behind your back.
With endless yearning
I breathe upon these dead ones here
that they may live.
Only a few of them dared
and lived for a short time.
I was of no use to the others.

Silent, I close my ears
to the scolding of the marketplace,
the terrible shrieks of the vendors.
I rarely cry out in anger,
and then I rebuke myself for letting it happen,
losing control.

I have to let things be,
to bear winter and summer in silence,
until that head breaks through, iridescent,
tender, red.

Nothing like it has ever
been seen before.

BIRDY

This too will be a past that gets farther
and farther away.
Two o'clock in the morning,
middle of November. This torment
will become summer and spring and winter,
a perfect circle—
will turn into a delicate scorching memory,
distorted.

I can already see before my eyes
the dead body withering to dust,
and rising out of it
—as if from the ocean waves,
from a seashell—
a rosy naked new woman.

The present will become a delusion
as water turns
into vapor.
And my head will be filled
like a red pomegranate
with delusions,
delusions,
and drift in the lofty heavens,
hollow, light,
dressed in feathers.

LIGHT AND DARKNESS

If you can dim the light,
skillfully
adjust the light,
the man in the window will again
be visible.
The man in that very high window,
I can't tell which floor,
with many layers of darkness beneath him.
The man is not asleep, of course.

And who's speaking now?
A woman who doesn't ordinarily
know happiness,
who doesn't please the mirror,
who's not at ease.
Wears glasses,
can't manage details.
It's not by chance
that I sit so long in the dark,
dim the lights,
leave the corners in darkness.

In the dark I see her sitting as I do,
closing the shutter in my face,
turning her back, pretending
she doesn't see.
She knows well enough
every motion of hers is visible to me.

The man in the window
comes from a distant land.
He's a wealthy man. Stays up all night, entertaining
that woman
he has just met.

Soon he'll push aside the drapes, look around
with satisfaction.
A foreign city lies before him.
He's had enough of foreign cities.
On his wrist, an accurate watch.
He knows that now, deep in the night, a woman
who has dimmed the lights
is sitting there, unseen.
She understands him.
He reads her thoughts.

They have a connection he shouldn't test
by coming any closer.
The two of them, wrapped in darkness like a blanket.
They're feeling fine.

THE WINDOW

And what have I done, after all?
For years I didn't do a thing.
I only looked out the window.
Raindrops soaked into the lawn,
year after year.
Blackbirds strolled across it.
Later, tiny flowers blossomed,
a chain of flowers,
probably in spring.
Then tulips, daffodils,
snapdragons,
nothing remarkable.
As for me, I did nothing.
Winter and summer tumbled
between the blades of grass.
I slept as much as I could.
It was a big enough window.
Whatever a person needs
I saw in that window.

NOTES TO THE POEMS

Hebrew words are stressed on the final syllable, unless otherwise indicated.

The Tearing
title: Refers to *kri'ah*, the Orthodox Jewish custom of making a tear in one's clothes as a sign of mourning.

The Commandment
epigraph: Based on Talmudic sayings. *Six hundred thirteen* is the traditional number of divine precepts *(mitzvot)* given to Israel; the *seven* given to the Sons of Noah are universal principles of ethics. *Even the dead:* Ravikovitch inverts the saying that the dead are exempt from the commandments.

The Land of the Setting Sun
epigraph: 2 Kings 23:11.

Night Sorrow
lines 20–21, *Return O my soul:* Ps. 116:7.

Around Jerusalem
lines 7–8, *the threshing-floor of the Jebusite:* 2 Sam. 24:18.

Behind the Rain
lines 1–3, *Kislev, Nisan, Tammuz:* Names of months in the Hebrew calendar. Kislev normally falls in November–December, Nisan in March–April, and Tammuz in June–July.

Requiem After Seventeen Years
lines 8–9, *the holy and pure:* Cf. the funeral prayer, *El Maleh Rahamim:* "O Lord, who art full of compassion, who dwellest on high, grant perfect rest to the deceased in the exalted places among the holy and pure, who shine as the brightness of the firmament."

Magic
lines 3–4, *like Mirian's well:* According to a Midrash based on

113

Num. 20–21, Miriam's well accompanied the children of Israel on their wanderings in the desert, providing them with water.

The Raging Waters
title: Cf. Ps. 65:7.
line 12, *I nearly went under:* Cf. Jonah 1:4.

Mahlon and Chilion
title: Naomi's two sons, who died in the land of Moab (Ruth 1:5). The names suggest "sickness" and "annihilation."

A Great Tremor
title: Cf. Isa. 22:17.
line 8, *Queen Tahpenes:* Wife of Pharaoh in the days of Solomon (1 Kings 11:19–20).
line 10, *The still waters of Shiloah:* Cf. Isa. 8:6.

The Horns of Hittin
title: Site of a celebrated battle near the Sea of Galilee, in which Saladin decisively defeated the Crusader armies in 1187.
line 35, *the Marquis of Montfort:* Conrad de Montferrat, one of the Crusader rulers of Jerusalem.
line 37, *his gloomy fortress:* The stronghold of Montfort, built to protect Acre; its ruins still stand today.

The End of the Fall
line 7, *blood is not the soul:* Here Ravikovitch inverts Deut. 12:23.

Even a Thousand Years
line 3, *Day unto day:* Ps. 19:2.
line 36, *a block of salt:* Alludes to Lot's wife (Gen. 19:26).
line 39, *potash and phosphate factory:* Located at the Dead Sea, traditionally the site of the destroyed cities of Sodom and Gomorrah (Gen. 19:24).

Day unto Day Uttereth Speech
title: Ps. 19:2.
line 16, *The heavens declare:* Ps. 19:1.

Poem of Explanations
lines 8–9, *rose of Sharon, lily of the valley:* Cant. 2:1.

Deep Calleth unto Deep
title: Ps. 42:7: "Deep calleth unto deep at the noise of thy waterspouts; all thy waves and thy billows are gone over me."
line 6, *I lifted my eyes to the hills:* Ps. 121:1.

In Jerusalem
line 3, *Ein Karem:* A village outside Jerusalem.

Like Rachel
line 1, *To die like Rachel:* Cf. Gen. 35:16–19.

King over Israel
line 28, *I, Koheleth:* Eccl. 1:12.
line 29, *How the city sat solitary:* Lam. 1:1.

Impoverishment
lines 10–11, *Waters without end:* Cf. Cant. 8:7.

The Sound of Birds at Noon
line 14, *to rule over day and night:* Gen. 1:16.

Iddo Wakes Up
line 20, *according to his will:* Echoes the words of a blessing said before eating certain foods: "Blessed art thou, O Lord our God, by whose will all things are created."

Cinderella in the Kitchen
line 23, *their necks outstretched:* Isa. 3:16.

The Finish Line
line 8, *He lifts his eyes:* Cf. Ps. 121:1.

Rough Draft
lines 12–13, *after a severe illness:* Alludes to the Hebrew poet Rachel [Blovstein] (1890–1931), who died of tuberculosis; in her poetry she associated herself with the biblical Rachel, who is also implied here (see "Like Rachel").

Blood Heifer
epigraph: added by the translators, abridging Deut. 21:1–9. The poem is based on an actual incident in which a yeshiva student was shot in the Hebron marketplace and left to die because no one knew his identity; the Jews assumed he was an Arab, and the Arabs, a Jew.

lines 31–33, *thine enemy's ass:* Ex. 23:5.

lines 36–37, *heifer...ashes:* Cf. also Num. 19.

You Can't Kill a Baby Twice
lines 1–2, *By the sewage puddles..., there:* Cf. Ps. 137:1.

lines 32–33, *to come home safe:* Echoes a line of a popular 1967 song about a war hero, now often quoted ironically to characterize the stock responses of returning soldiers.

On the Attitude toward Children in Wartime
This is a variation on a poem by Natan Zach that deals satirically with the question of whether there were exaggerations in the number of children reported killed in the war in Lebanon [Note by D.R.].

lines 1–2, *He who destroys:* Echoes a familiar Mishnaic saying: "He who destroys a single soul of Israel, it is as if he had destroyed the entire universe."

lines 16–17, *As when a man runs away:* Amos 5:19.

Hovering at a Low Altitude
lines 18–19, *neck outstretched, wanton glances:* Isa. 3:16.

line 20, *Whence cometh my help:* Ps. 121:1.

New Zealand
lines 9, 30, *He maketh me...green pastures:* Ps. 23:2.

It Will Certainly Come
line 20, *I breathe upon these dead:* Cf. Ezek. 37:9.

Birdy
title: An American film.

BIOGRAPHICAL NOTES

Dahlia Ravikovitch was born in 1936 in Ramat Gan, a suburb of Tel Aviv. She studied at the Hebrew University in Jerusalem, and later worked as a journalist and teacher. She has published five volumes of poetry, *The Love of an Orange, A Hard Winter, The Third Book, Deep Calleth Unto Deep,* and *Real Love;* a book of selected poems, *All Thy Breakers and Waves;* a book of short stories, *A Death in the Family;* and two books of poetry for children, *Family Party* and *Mixed-Up Mommy*. She is the recipient of many of Israel's literary awards: the Shlonsky, Brenner, Ussishkin and Bialik Prizes, as well as the Award of the Municipality of Ramat Gan. She now lives in Tel Aviv with her husband and son, and writes television reviews for the newspaper *Ma'ariv*.

Chana Bloch is Professor of English Literature and Chairman of the English Department at Mills College. She has published a book of poems, *The Secrets of the Tribe;* a critical study, *Spelling the Word: George Herbert and the Bible;* and two volumes of translations from Hebrew, *A Dress of Fire: Poems by Dahlia Ravikovitch* and (in collaboration with Stephen Mitchell) *Selected Poetry of Yehuda Amichai*. Her awards include the Discovery Award and the Poets & Writers Exchange Award and an NEA award for her poetry, a National Endowment for the Humanities Fellowship and the Book of the Year Award of the Conference on Christianity and Literature for her criticism, and the Columbia University Translation Center Award.

Ariel Bloch is Professor of Semitic Linguistics at the University of California at Berkeley. Most of his books and articles deal with Arabic and Hebrew syntax and semantics. The books are *Damaszenisch-Arabische Texte, Die Hypotaxe im Damaszenisch-Arabischen, A Chrestomathy of Modern Literary Arabic,* and *Studies in Arabic Syntax and Semantics*. Among his awards are a National Endowment for the Humanities Senior Fellowship, the President of the University of California's Research Fellowship in the Humanities, and a National Science Foundation grant.